Rails Across The Isle Of Man

in the 1950s

Adrian Kennedy

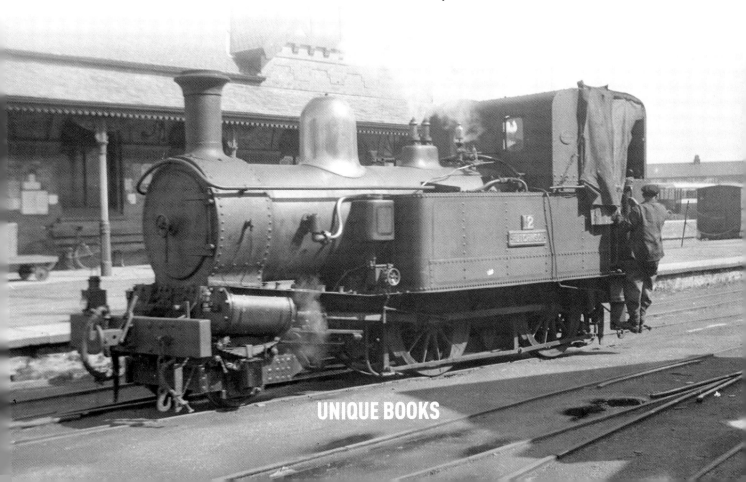

UNIQUE BOOKS

Front cover: Isle of Man Railway No 1 *Sutherland* is pictured bringing in the stock for the 2.15pm to Ramsey at St John's on 1 August 1953. *John McCann/Online Transport Archive*

Previous page: The southern terminus of the Isle of Man Railway – Port Erin – pictured on 8 April 1950 as 2-4-0T No 12 *Hutchinson* runs round its train after arrival from Douglas. This locomotive was built by Beyer Peacock in 1908 and was named after William Hutchinson, who was a local politician and director of the railway. No 12 was one of only two locomotives – the other being No 5 – that carried cast numbers above the name plate on the side of the tanks. Following Nationalisation, No 12 was given a new Hunslet-built boiler with slightly enlarged tanks; it remained in this condition until returned to original condition. The locomotive is, at the time of writing, out of service and is scheduled to receive one of the new boilers being constructed by the Severn Valley Railway for the line. *Tony Wickens/Online Transport Archive*

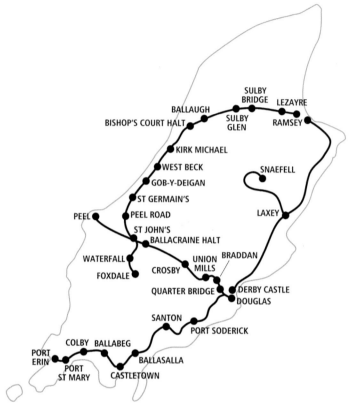

Rails across the Isle of Man in the 1950s

Adrian Kennedy

First published in the United Kingdom by Unique Books 2021

© Text: Author 2021
© Photographs: As credited

ISBN: 978 1 913555 05 4

All rights reserved. No part of this book may be reproduced or transmitted in any form or by any means electronic or mechanical, including photocopying, recording or by any information storage without permission from the Publisher in writing. All enquiries should be directed to the Publisher.

A CIP record for this book is available from the British Library

Unique Books is an imprint of Unique Publishing Services Ltd, 3 Merton Court, The Strand, Brighton Marina Village, Brighton BN2 5XY.

www.uniquebooks.pub

Printed in India

A note on the photographs
All of the illustrations in this book have been drawn from the collection of the Online Transport Archive, a UK-registered charity that was set up to accommodate collections put together by transport enthusiasts who wished to see their precious images secured for the long-term. Further information about the archive can be found at: www.onlinetransportarchive.org or email secretary@onlinetransportarchive.org

INTRODUCTION

During the 1950s, the Isle of Wight could claim that it had perhaps the most concentrated variety of historic public transport within the British Isles. There was the only surviving horse tramway – the 3ft 0in-gauge route along the promenade in Douglas from Victoria Pier to Derby Castle – plus the two electric tramways – the 3ft 0in-gauge Manx Electric and the 3ft 6in-gauge Snaefell Mountain railways – as well as the extensive steam-operated network operated by the 3ft 0in-gauge Isle of Man Railway. In addition, the last remains of the Douglas Southern Electric Tramway – the only standard gauge line built on the island – were still extant whilst the Ramsey Pier Railway and the Groudle Glen Railway were still operational as was the last of the cliff funiculars.

Much of this infrastructure dated back to the late 19th century when the island developed as a major destination for holidaymakers and when there was some attempts to exploit the island's mineral wealth. By the 1950s, however, there was evidence that the numbers of annual visitors were in decline. The Douglas Southern Electric Tramway had suspended operation at the outbreak of war in September 1939 and services were never restored. The zoo at Groudle Glen was another casualty; whilst the railway continued to operate through the decade – albeit largely reduced to a single working locomotive – one of its prime attractions had disappeared.

On the steam railway, two of the 16 surviving steam locomotives after the war soon disappeared: No 7 *Tynwald*, which had been damaged in a collision with No 10 *G.H.Wood* in 1928 and never repaired, was withdrawn in 1947 (although some parts were stored thereafter and the frames were purchased for preservation and still survive, now being stored at the Southwold Railway in East Anglia), whilst No 2 *Derby*, one of the original locomotives acquired from Beyer Peacock in 1873, was withdrawn and scrapped in 1951 in order to provide spares for the other locomotives.

The 1950s represented the last decade when the Isle of Man Railway's network remained largely intact although the Foxdale branch was to disappear by the end of the decade. Lead traffic from Foxdale had ceased in 1911 and the line had remained open thereafter for the limited passenger services and general freight until 16 May 1940 when the former had ceased. Limited freight traffic continued until the late 1950s with the last train – an engineering working – running in January 1960. The track largely remained after closure for more than a decade but was lifted during the 1970s.

By the early 1960s, the railway's financial position deteriorated with the Ramsey line in particular becoming increasingly loss making. Efforts were made during the late 1950s and early 1960s to improve the finances – such as the purchase of the redundant County Donegal diesel railcars in 1961 and service reductions – but these merely delayed the day of reckoning. The entire system closed at the end of the 1965 season – winter services had been suspended some years earlier to save money – and was only revived for 1967 through the intervention of the Marquess of Ailsa. Although services to Peel, Ramsey and Port Erin operated for the next two summers, the end of the 1968 season saw the final closure to passengers of the Peel and Ramsey lines. The Port Erin line continued to struggle and was finally nationalised in 1978.

The Manx Electric and the Snaefell Mountain railways were also to struggle financially through the immediate post-war years. The company was nationalised in 1957. The new owners brought some much needed investment to the line with track being relayed between Derby Castle and Laxey. Less positive was the introduction of a new green and white livery that was highly unpopular and destined to last only a few years. The importance of the Snaefell line was increased after 1950 when the Air Ministry opened a radar station at its peak; the use of the railway for winter maintenance saw the introduction of a series of diesel railcars for use in the winter months. Both lines survived intact through the decade but, increasingly, there was a threat to the line north of Laxey. This was exacerbated by the loss of the mail contract in 1975 and operation of the section north of Laxey was suspended briefly.

More than six decades on from the views in this book, the Isle of Man remains a fascinating destination for the enthusiast but, as recorded here, much has also sadly disappeared over the intervening years.

With the attractive station building in the background, No 11 *Maitland* stands in Port Erin station as passengers board the three-coach train on 8 April 1950. The locomotive was one of two locomotives delivered from Beyer Peacock in 1905 – the other being No 10 (the two being the first 'medium' boilered locomotives to be constructed) – and No 11 was named after Dalrymple Maitland, who was a director of the railway and a local politician. Reboilered in 1959, No 11 was to be one of the mainstays of the railway through the Marquess of Ailsa era and the early period of nationalisation. Withdrawn in 1978 a further reboilering saw the locomotive re-enter service in 1981. Withdrawn again in 2007, the locomotive is expected to re-enter service in 2021 fitted with a new boiler built by the Severn Valley Railway and following work at Alan Keef Ltd. The first carriage in the set is No F49; this was the last of 12 'Large Fs' constructed by the Metropolitan Carriage & Wagon Co between 1925 and 1926. Of the 12, five – including No F49 (which is undergoing a rebuild at the time of writing) – remain part of the operational fleet, one is stored and the underframes of three more are also still extant. The remaining three (plus the bodies of the three surviving underframes) were all scrapped between 1976 and 1983. A number of those scrapped were victims of the fire at St John's that saw a number of wooden-bodied coaches destroyed in 1975.
Tony Wickens/Online Transport Archive

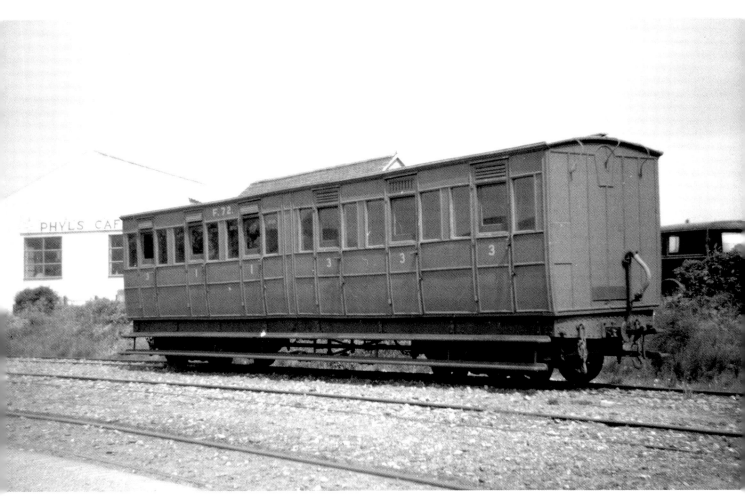

On 9 June 1956 carriage No F72 awaits its next duty at Port Erin. From 1887 the railway's original four-wheel stock was close-coupled in pairs to reduce the length of trains. Between 1909 and 1926 bodies of a number of these carriages were removed from their original frames and mounted on new bogie underframes supplied by the Metropolitan Carriage & Wagon Co. These coaches – Nos F50-F75 – were known as 'Pairs' and No F72 – converted in 1926 – was amongst the last to be so treated. By the late 1950s, the type was increasingly rare in normal service due to age, although they were used for school traffic and on days of exceptional traffic need. Today a handful remain operational with others in store; of the 26 carriages, 11 remain with the railway. The body of No F72 was scrapped in 1967 although its underframe – and that of a number of others – was sold to the Ffestiniog Railway and can now be found under FR coach No 117. *Marcus Eavis/Online Transport Archive*

A Port Erin-bound train is seen entering Castletown station during August 1956. The station opened with the Douglas to Port Erin line on 1 August 1874 and was provided with a stone-built main building; this was built in locally sourced limestone from Scarlett Pointon. The original station was enlarged in 1903 with canopy and veranda added seven years later.
Phil Tatt/Online Transport Archive

On 11 June 1956 the 4.15pm service is pictured awaiting departure from Ballasalla station. The station opened on 1 August 1874 when it was provided with a wooden station building on the northbound platform as illustrated in this view; this building survived until 1985 when it was replaced by the brick-built building that is still extant today. The station was also provided with two passenger platforms – as with a number of stations on the Isle of Man Railway the ground-level platform have been replaced with raised platforms; the northbound platform was modified in the late 1980s and the southbound in 2002.
Julian Thompson/Online Transport Archive

When opened on 1 August 1874 Port Soderick was provided with a fairly basic station; however, the facilities were to prove inadequate to cater for the crowds visiting the nearby resort with the result that a more substantial station building – seen here from the train on 8 April 1950 – was constructed in 1898. This structure incorporated a stationmaster's house and refreshment rooms. Although the building is still extant, it is now a private residence and the station is unmanned. A further change over the past 70 years is the provision of raised platforms on both the up and down sides.
Tony Wickens/Online Transport Archive

On 9 June 1956 Isle of Man Railway Nos 13 *Kissack* and 10 *G. H. Wood* stand in Douglas station. The former was built by Beyer Peacock and was new in 1910. Named after Edward Thomas Kissack, who was a director of the line and a local politician, No 13 was to be withdrawn the same year and was to remain in store until 1971 when it was restored to service. Now reboilered, No 13 is still part of the steam railway's operational fleet. No 10 was new in 1905 and named after George Henry Wood, who was the railway's company secretary. No 10 was to survive in service until withdrawal with a defective boiler in 1977. It was repaired and returned to service in 1993. At the time of writing it is currently out of service, its boiler certificate having expired in August 2017, for overhaul.
Marcus Eavis/Online Transport Archive

Following the take-over of the Manx Northern Railway in 1905, the Isle of Man Railway acquired six bogie coaches – Nos F29-32/35/36 – from the Metropolitan Carriage & Wagon Co to replace the MNR's six-wheel coaches. These were the first to be built with wooden bodies on steel underframes. On 13 June 1956 two of the sextet – Nos F31 and F32 – are seen in Douglas station. All bar No F36 remain active; the one exception, which has been used as the royal saloon, is now preserved in the Isle of Man Railway Museum, where it has been based since 1976. The remaining five have been modified by the addition of corridor connections; Nos F31, F32 and F35 underwent this modification in 1981 as part of the conversion to a three-carriage bar set.
Julian Thompson/Online Transport Archive

For the opening of the Isle of Man Railway in 1873, Beyer Peacock supplied three 2-4-0Ts. The first of these – No 1 *Sutherland* – is pictured here receiving treatment from the crew at Douglas station during the summer of 1953. The locomotive was named after George Sutherland-Leveson-Gower, 3rd Duke of Sutherland, who was prominent in the development of the Highland Railway in Scotland – particularly on the route north of Inverness – as well as being a director of the Isle of Man Railway. No 1 remained in service until 1964 before spending the next 30 years on display; however, it was restored to steam in 1998 – using the restored boiler from No 8 *Fenella* – as part of the celebrations for the 125th anniversary of the line. It retained this boiler until 2003 when No 8 was restored to service. No 1 was then put back into store until 2018 when it was cosmetically restored prior to being returned to the railway's museum in 2020.
John McCann/Online Transport Archive

The last of the 2-4-0Ts supplied to the railway, and the most powerful, by Beyer Peacock was No 16 *Mannin*, which was new in 1926. This was acquired in order to be able to haul the Port Erin boat train – which had previously required double-heading or banking – with a single locomotive. As a consequence, it was significantly larger than the earlier 2-4-0Ts. Withdrawn from service in 1964 and placed on static display with plans later in the decade for its restoration rejected as a result of its non-standard design, No 16 was displayed in the line's railway museum in 1975. However, in early 2020 No 16 was removed from the museum with a view to restoring it to an operational condition for the 150th anniversary of the line's opening in 2023.
John McCann/Online Transport Archive

In order to increase the railway's locomotive fleet prior to the opening of the line to Port Erin, Beyer Peacock supplied two new locomotives – Nos 4 *Loch* and 5 *Mona* – in 1874. No 5, which is named after the Roman name for the island, received a larger boiler in 1911 and remained in service until the end of the 1969 season. Note the brass numeral on the side of the tank; No 5, pictured here at Douglas, was one of only two locomotives so adorned – the other being No 12 – on the left-hand side tank only. Privately preserved in 1978 – but still stored on the railway (originally in the carriage shed until the building was demolished in 1999 and now in the new carriage shed) – No 5 has received little attention since withdrawal.
John McCann/Online Transport Archive

During the summer of 1953 No 3 *Pender* is seen shunting at Douglas. No 3 was the third of the original batch of locomotives and was built by Beyer Peacock in 1873; named after Sir John Pender, who was a director of the company, No 3 was withdrawn in 1962 and was to be cannibalised for spare parts. The remains were acquired in 1977 and returned to England; the locomotive is now on display in sectionalised form at the Science & Industry Museum in Manchester.
John McCann/Online Transport Archive

During the summer of 1953, No 10 *G. H. Wood* stands alongside the platform at Braddan Halt as passengers disembark from the train. A second service can be seen in the distance awaiting access to the platform. The halt here was opened in 1897 and was generally used only infrequently, often in conjunction with open-air church services held on Sundays during the summer months at nearby Kirk Braddan. Once the passengers had disembarked, the train would run through to Union Mills, where the locomotive would run round the stock prior to returning to Braddan Halt to pick up the passengers for the return journey. The station closed finally with the line on 7 September 1968 and the track was lifted in the mid-1970s. The wooden booking office and passenger shelter survived, however, and in 1991 was restored and transferred to the still operational station at Colby.
John McCann/Online Transport Archive

During the summer of 1953 No 8 *Fenella* is pictured awaiting departure from St John's with a service towards Douglas. Named after a character in Sir Walter Scott's novel *Peveril of the Peak*, No 8 was delivered in 1894 and was allocated for many years to services on the line to Ramsey. Withdrawn during the Marquess of Ailsa's control of the line, No 8 was sold in 1978 with a view to restoration. The boiler was sent to Bridgnorth on the Severn Valley Railway for overhaul with work being completed in 1998; between 1998 and 2003 the boiler was used to permit No 1 *Sutherland* to return to steam. The boiler was subsequently returned to No 8, which has operated on the surviving Port Erin section since 2004 (except largely between 2008 and 2012). It returned to the railway's ownership in 2012. Behind the locomotive is carriage No F4; this was one of six bogie coaches – Nos F1-F6 – that were supplied by Brown Marshall & Co Ltd in 1876. These were the first of the 'Small F' type – so named because they were, at 35ft 0in in length and 9ft 6in in height, smaller than subsequent deliveries. In all 26 'Small Fs' were delivered between 1876 and 1896; of the initial batch, four, including No 4, were scrapped in 1976 leaving two to be preserved. Of the 26 built, four remain in operational condition.
John McCann/Online Transport Archive

Built by Beyer Peacock for the Manx Northern Railway, No 14 *Thornhill* was MNR No 3 becoming Isle of Man Railway No 14 when the two railways merged in 1905. It was named after the home of the MNR's chairman Thornhill House. The MNR's first two locomotives – Nos 1 *Ramsey* and 2 *Northern* – were supplied by Sharp Stewart & Co in 1880. These two 2-4-0Ts were allocated the numbers 16 and 17 after the merger but were little used thereafter and were scrapped in 1923 and 1912 respectively. No 14 lost its chimney numerals in 1956 when it was given a replacement chimney and was to remain in service until 1963, largely in original condition and retaining its Salter safety valves. Displayed statically at St John's in the late 1960s, it was sold for preservation in 1978. Although still based on the island, it is not on public display. It is pictured here at St John's awaiting departure with the first of the 'Small Fs' – No F26 – in the background.
John McCann/Online Transport Archive

Pictured taking water at St John's is No 9 *Douglas*. Built by Beyer Peacock at Gorton Foundry and new in 1896, No 9 was named after the island's capital and was purchased to help the railway cater for the growing traffic. When recorded here the locomotive, which had been reboilered in 1912, was approaching the end of its career as it was withdrawn in late 1953. Stored thereafter and displayed for a period in the late 1960s, No 9 was sold in 1978 although remaining on the railway. During 2020 the locomotive was dismantled and asbestos removed with additional work being undertaken. Having been painted in red primer, the locomotive's boiler is at the time of writing stored at Douglas with the frames, wheels and superstructure stored at Port Erin.
Marcus Eavis/Online Transport Archive

Seen outside the carriage shed at St John's during August 1956 is luggage van No F28. This was one of two bogie vans – the other being No F27 – that were built by the Metropolitan Carriage & Wagon Co and new in 1897; the delivery year, being Queen Victoria's Golden Jubilee, resulted in the duo being known as 'Empress Vans'. Over the years, the pair saw a variety of uses – including acting as ambulances during the annual TT races – until 1992 when both were taken out of service and stored in the open. The body of No F27 was scrapped in 2012 and its frames stored; No F28 remains in store at Douglas at the time of writing.
Phil Tatt/Online Transport Archive

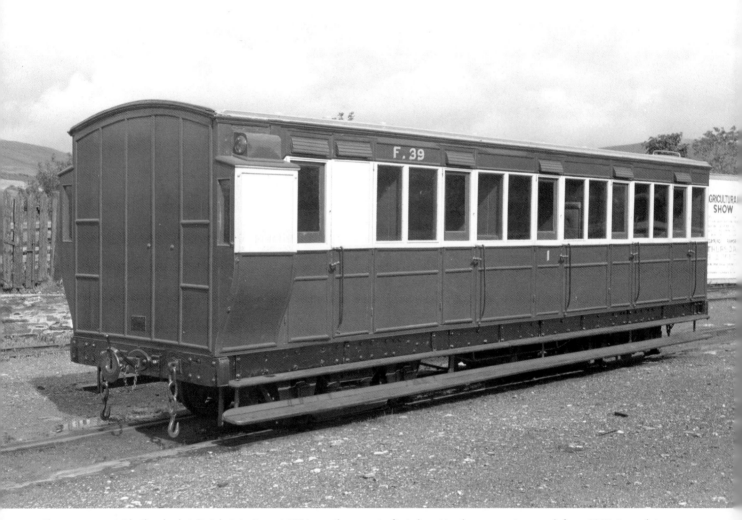

Also present outside the shed at St John's in August 1956 was the unique No F39. Built by the Oldbury Carriage & Wagon Co and new in 1887, the bogie carriage – the shortest on the railway at 30ft 0in – was built for the Foxdale Railway. When new, it had four third-class compartments along with a small guard's compartment; subsequently, one of the third-class compartments was converted to first class. Used as a camping coach from 1967, it was later restored to passenger use and remains operational with the railway. It is currently painted Manx Northern Railway livery and bears its MNR No 17.
Phil Tatt/Online Transport Archive

With the Manx Northern Railway initially being operated from opening in 1879 by the Isle of Man Railway, services from Ramsey operated to the latter's station in St John's. However, with the Manx Northern taking over operation the following year, a separate station was built. This lasted until 1884 when a new station – illustrated here on 8 April 1950 – was built on the alignment under construction for the new Foxdale branch. After amalgamation, services to and from Ramsey reverted to using the original IoMR station with the MNR station being used solely for services on the branch until 1927. Thereafter, until the withdrawal of passenger services, trains on the branch made use of the IoMR station by reversing into and out of it. In 1906 the MNR station was converted into a house for the stationmaster. The building survives as a private residence.
Tony Wickens/Online Transport Archive

The Foxdale branch was promoted by the Foxdale Railway Co and opened on 16 August 1886 primarily to serve the district's lead mines. The line shared directors with the Manx Northern although the two companies were separate. The Foxdale Railway Co was forced into liquidation five years after it opened as a result of the decline in the lead industry; operation was then handled by the Manx Northern on behalf of the liquidators until the Isle of Man Railway assumed operation of both the MNR and the Foxdale branch on 26 February 1904; ownership of both passed to the IoMR on 9 April 1905. When recorded here on 8 April 1950, it was almost a decade after the last regular passenger services to Foxdale had operated. These had been replaced by buses and, when the buses failed occasionally, a passenger train ran in place. There had also been some limited operation for servicemen during World War 2. The last recorded train operated in January 1960 and, thereafter, the line was moribund although it was not lifted until the 1970s. The station remains extant whilst the trackbed towards St John's is a public footpath.
Tony Wickens/Online Transport Archive

On 11 June 1956 No 6 *Peveril* is seen about one mile short of its destination with the 10.30am from Douglas to Peel. Named after the title character in Sir Walter Scott's novel *Peveril of the Peak*, No 6 was withdrawn in August 1960. Displayed as a static exhibit at St John's during 1967 and subsequently at Douglas station, No 6 was retained in store in the carriage shed at Douglas until it was removed for cosmetic restoration by the Isle of Man Steam Railway Supporters' Association. After this work was completed, the locomotive was put on display at the railway museum in Port Erin. It remained there until 2020 when it was removed and partially dismantled to facilitate asbestos removal. It remains, at the time of writing, in a partially dismantled condition in the carriage shed at Port Erin.
Marcus Eavis/Online Transport Archive

No 4 *Loch* pictured at Peel on 8 April 1950. Built by Beyer Peacock in 1874, No 4 was named after Henry Brougham Loch, who served as Lieutenant Governor of the Isle of Man from 1863 until 1882 (when he was appointed Governor of Victoria in Australia). When new, No 4 was equipped with a small boiler but it was rebuilt as medium boilered locomotive in 1909. Taken out of service in 1955, the locomotive was undergoing a reboilering during 1967 with the intention that it would re-enter service during 1968. The closure of the lines to Peel and Ramsey in September 1968 coincided with the completion of the locomotive's repair and it remained in service on the Douglas-Port Erin line until 1995 when it was again withdrawn. Operated, following repair, between 2002 and 2015, the locomotive has recently undergone a further boiler overhaul and was due to re-enter service in 2020.
Tony Wickens/Online Transport Archive

No 10 *G. H. Wood* is pictured again, this time in the terminus at Peel in June 1956. Although the Isle of Man Railway initially planned to construct the line from St John's to run through Peel to Ramsey, when the decision was made to terminate the route at Peel the location of the proposed station was moved to a site adjacent to the harbour. The line opened on 1 July 1873. Along with the rest of the IoMR, the line to Peel was suspended between November 1965 and June 1967, when services were reintroduced under the auspices of the Marquess of Alisa. However, final closure to passenger traffic came on 6 September 1968. The track was lifted in 1975 with the remains of the engine shed demolished at the same time. The goods shed, however, survives having been converted to house originally a replica Viking longship in 1979; the shed and the main station building now form part of the heritage centre the House of Manannan, which opened in 1997.
Julian Thompson/Online Transport Archive

In August 1956 No 6 *Peveril* heads westbound heading inland from St Germain's towards St John's during August 1956. With the failure of the Isle of Man Railway to construct a line to serve Ramsey, a separate railway was promoted. Construction on the 16½-mile long Manx Northern line from St John's to Ramsey commenced in 1878 and the route was opened throughout on 23 September 1879. Initially operated by the Isle of Man Railway, the MNR took over operation itself on 6 November 1880. The following year, exercising running powers over the line south from St John's the MNR introduced through services to Douglas. The company maintained an independent existence until 1905 when it was formally taken over by the Isle of Man Railway.
Phil Tatt/Online Transport Archive

With Peel in the background No 10 *G. H. Wood* heads eastbound on 1 August 1953 at Gob Y Deigan with the 12 noon service from Douglas to Ramsey.
John McCann/Online Transport Archive

On 11 June 1956 the 1.45pm service from Ramsey to Douglas is pictured crossing Glen Wyllin viaduct. The western part of the Manx Northern Railway required some significant engineering work including the construction of two viaducts – this one and that Glen Mooar – on the section between St Germain's and Kirk Michael stations. Following the cessation of all traffic to Ramsey, with the withdrawal of the fuel oil trains in April 1969, the track from St John's to Ramsey was lifted in 1974 and the two viaducts were dismantled the following year.
Marcus Eavis/Online Transport Archive

The exterior of Ramsey station viewed from the south on 11 June 1956. As the terminus and headquarters of the Manx Northern Railway, a substantial single-storey station was constructed for the line's opening on 23 September 1879. The station was also provided with a goods yard with cattle dock whilst a short branch ran from the north of the yard to the town's harbour. By the 1950s passenger traffic over the line from St John's to Ramsey was in decline and, from 1960, the service became seasonal. Following the final passenger services on 6 September 1968 there was limited fuel oil traffic until April 1969. The track remained intact it was removed in 1975. Following the closure of the line, the station building was eventually demolished and a bakery constructed on the site.
Marcus Eavis/Online Transport Archive

As passengers wait in the background, 'Winter Saloon' No 20 is shunted at the MER's Ramsey terminus. The northern extension from Laxey was opened as far as Ballure on 2 August 1898; it was not until 24 July 1899 that the final link into Ramsey itself was opened. Now complete, the route from Douglas to Ramsey ran for some 17 miles.
F. E. J. Ward/Online Transport Archive

For much of its life the Manx Electric Railway carried both passengers and freight traffic and, for the latter work, it employed a number of wagons. No 3 – pictured here at Ramsey during 1953 – was one of two six-ton closed vans supplied to the line by G. F. Milnes & Co in December 1894. When seen here, the wagon was painted in grey with black lettering and is in original condition; over the winter of 1963/64 the wagon lost its end platforms.

Withdrawn in the late 1970s, No 3 was stored at Laxey from 1978 until 2002 when it was transferred to the Homefield bus depot in Douglas. It remained there until 2009 when it relocated to Dhoon Quarry for further storage; recovered the following year, No 3 is currently undergoing restoration. Sister wagon No 4 is operational and has been painted bright red since 1993 and is used for special events on the line. *John McCann/Online Transport Archive*

Two more of the MER's freight stock recorded at Ramsey during August 1953. On the left is open wagon No 7 and on the right van No 13. The former was a six-ton open wagon that was supplied by G. F. Milnes & Co in 1897 to assist in the extension of the line from Laxey to Ballure. It was to survive in use by the Permanent Way Department until the late 1970s before being scrapped. It was one of five similar vehicles – Nos 6-10 – of which two survive with the railway. No 13 was one of two small vans built by G. F. Milnes & Co and new during 1903/04. Overhauled in the late 1950s, it survived in service until 1979 and has been in store ever since. At present it is located at Dhoon Quarry. Sister vehicle No 14, which was described as a 'luggage van' when new in 1904, was converted into a flat wagon with its body being scrapped in 2002. Like No 13, it is currently stored in the open at Dhoon Quarry.
Phil Tatt/Online Transport Archive

On 10 June 1956 MER No 19 ascends Walpole Road, Ramsey, with a service towards Douglas. Note the groved rail; at the time this was the only section of the line to be so equipped. No 19 was one of four cars – Nos 19-22 – known as 'Winter Saloons' that were supplied by G. F. Milnes & Co in 1899 in readiness for the opening of the line from Laxey to Ramsey. All were equipped with Brill 27Cx bogies. No 19 was to be slightly damaged in a fire at Derby Castle in 1992; sister car No 22 was destroyed in the same incident (albeit rebuilt as a replica). All four remain in operational condition on the line.
Julian Thompson/Online Transport Archive

Pictured looking north at Dhoon Glen on 12 June 1956, 'Winter Saloon' No 21 is seen heading towards Laxey. The northern extension from Laxey to Ramsey was authorised in May 1897 and the line was opened – as far as Ballure – by the then Lieutenant Governor, John Henniker-Major, on 2 August 1898. The investment in the extension to Ramsey, which left the line (then owned by the Isle of Man Tramways & Electric Power Co) in debt to the tune of £150,000 (equivalent to about £19½ million in 2020), led to financial crisis and the liquidation of the company. Its assets were acquired in 1902 and the company was reborn as the Manx Electric Railway.
Julian Thompson/Online Transport Archive

To the south of Dhoon Glen, the Manx Electric is sandwiched between the main A2 road from Laxey north to Ramsey and the cliffs of Bulgham Bay and it is on this section that 'Winter Saloon' No 19 and a trailer are seen heading south on 12 June 1956. By the mid-1960s the future of the line north of Laxey was open to some debate as the MER's finances deteriorated. The issues were to become even more significant on 23 January 1967 when coastal erosion caused a section of the line above Bulgham bay to collapse, thus severing the line. Services were maintained both north and south of the line whilst the track was repaired but it was not until 10 July 1967 that through services were restored. The threat to the line was again highlighted in October 1975 when the MER lost its contract with the Post Office to transport mail. This resulted in the suspension of services north of Laxey; they were not restored until the summer of 1977.
Julian Thompson/Online Transport Archive

For the opening of the Snaefell Mountain Railway G. F. Milnes & Co Ltd supplied six single-deck 3ft 6in gauge trams; these were equipped with bogies supplied by the same company. In August 1953, Nos 1 and 2 are seen at the Laxey terminus. Both remain in service although No 1 underwent a significant restoration during 2011 and 2012 when it reverted to the original blue – as opposed to red – teak and white livery with the first name – 'Snaefell Mountain Tramway' – along its side panels.
Phil Tatt/Online Transport Archive

Snaefell No 2 is seen again, this time as it descends towards Laxey and the connection with the Manx Electric Railway. This angle gives a good perspective on the Fell third rail with which the five-mile long line is equipped. Developed by John Barraclough Fell and initially tested on a section of the Cromford & High Peak line in Derbyshire during the early 1860s, the Fell system was one of a number of innovations developed during the latter half of the 19th century to enable railways and tramways to ascend (and descend) safely lines where adhesion alone was not adequate. The Snaefell line, which was eventually built entirely on private land (and so did not require statutory powers for its construction), was originally surveyed by Fell's son, George Noble Fell, and anticipated the use of steam. These original proposals of 1888 were not progressed but the line – built to a slightly different alignment – was ultimately promoted by the Snaefell Mountain Railway Association in 1895; construction was rapid and the line opened throughout on 20 August 1895.
Phil Tatt/Online Transport Archive

Pictured at the Summit terminus of the Snaefell Mountain Railway on 10 June 1956 is No 5. Although the line operated with its original fleet of six cars for more than 70 years, No 5 was the first to be withdrawn when it was destroyed by fire on 16 August 1970. Although the car was rebuilt using its original Milnes-built bogies, there were detailed differences between the body of the 'new' car and the remaining older cars although these have been reduced over the years by subsequent modifications. More recently, a second car – No 3 – has also been withdrawn following an incident on 30 March 2016 when it ran away from the Summit terminus and was derailed. The remains of No 3 remain in store with the intention, in due course, of it being rebuilt.
Julian Thompson/Online Transport Archive

In 1950 the Air Ministry established a radar station on Snaefell in 1950. In order to gain access the summit to maintain the station during the winter months, when the overhead on the upper section of the line was removed, a Wickham was acquired in 1951. Painted in RAF blue, the Wickham trolley – seen here on 19 May 1956 – survived in service until 1977 when it was transferred to the MER; it was to pass into preservation in the UK during 2007. Since 1951, the Air Ministry and its successors (the Civil Aviation Authority and National Air Traffic Services) have employed four different Wickham trolleys; the most recent arrived in 1991.
M. J. Lea/LRTA (London Area) Collection/Online Transport Archive

With No 33 preparing to run round prior to heading south back to Douglas, trailer No 61 stands at Laxey in August 1953. In 1906 the United Electric Car Co supplied two new crossbench cars – Nos 32 and 33 – that were fitted with Brill 27Cx bogies and two unpowered trailers – Nos 61 and 62. Nos 32 and 33 were, when new, the most powerful trams operational on the line. Although they were capable of hauling two trailers if required, this was rarely necessary. All four cars are currently operational. The extension of the Douglas & Laxey Coast Electric Tramway Co's line from Groudle Glen to Laxey, on which construction started in February 1894, was opened on 28 July of the same year.
Phil Tatt/Online Transport Archive

Viewed from the west, a crossbench tram and trailer head south over the stone-built viaduct south of Laxey with a Douglas-bound service on 10 June 1956. The original terminus of the line from Douglas was situated next to Lower Rencell Road. The four-arch viaduct across the Glen Roy valley was constructed in 1897 as part of project to extend the line northwards to Ramsey.
Julian Thompson/Online Transport Archive

With Laxey Head in the distance and the beach at Laxey Bay prominent, 'Winter Saloon' No 21 and a trailer head southbound towards Douglas on 12 June 1956. The small harbour at Laxey was developed in the 1850s to transport material produced by the local mining industry; although this traffic has now ceased, the harbour remains in use for fishing and leisure sailing. Laxey Bay is now a protected Marine Nature Reserve.
Julian Thompson/Online Transport Archive

Heading north towards Laxey at Garwick Glen with a service from Douglas in August 1953 are power car No 16 and trailer No 46. The former was one of five crossbench cars – Nos 14-18 – supplied by G. F. Milnes & Co in 1898; all were fitted with the same manufacturer's S3 bogies with the exception of No 16, which was equipped by bogies supplied by Brush. Of the five, Nos 14 and 16 remain operational with the remaining three in store; No 17 was slightly damaged in the 1990 fire that destroyed No 22. No 46 was one of a quartet – Nos 45-48 – of trailers supplied by G. F. Milnes & Co in 1899. All four remain operational although No 45 lost its body in 2003 when it was converted into a flat wagon for works duties. *Phil Tatt/Online Transport Archive*

With the station in the background, No 7 and crossbench trailer No 40 depart from Garwick Glen northbound towards Laxey during August 1953. Three trailer cars – Nos 40, 41 and 44 – were destroyed alongside a number of motor cars in the disastrous Laxey depot fire of 1930. Whilst none of the latter were replaced, three new trailers were constructed by English Electric at Preston to replace those lost in the fire. Although the bodies built were wholly new, the three cars were fitted with the original unpowered Milnes-built S1 bogies salvaged from the destroyed cars. All three remain in serviceable condition on the line.
Phil Tatt/Online Transport Archive

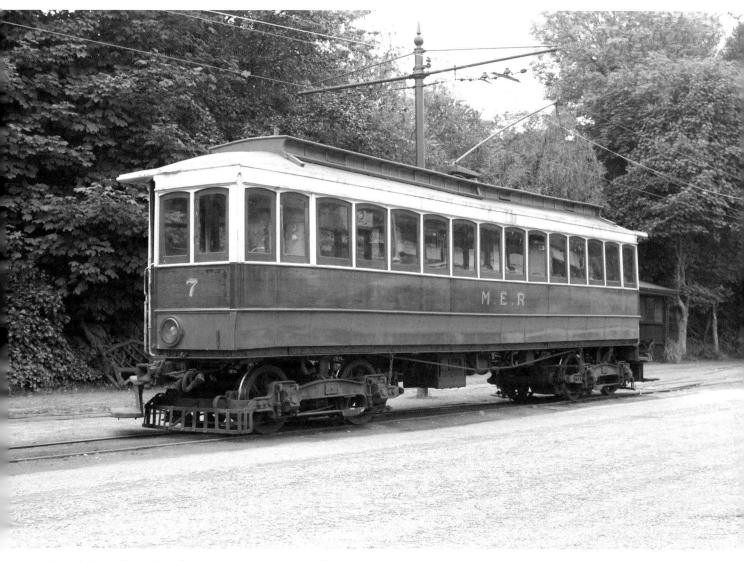

Recorded standing at Groudle Glen during the summer of 1956 is No 7. This was one of six power cars – Nos 4-9 – that were supplied by G. F. Milnes & Co for the opening of the line to Laxey in 1894. Fitted with enclosed platform vestibules from new, the type became known as 'Tunnel' cars as a result of their longitudinal seating. Two of the batch – Nos 4 and 8 – were destroyed in the Laxey depot fire of 1930. No 7 was used, for a number of years, as a works car and its condition deteriorated. In 2010 it underwent a major restoration to restore it to passenger service; this was completed the following year. It, along with Nos 5 and 9 remain operational. The first section of the future Manx Electric Railway – from Douglas to Groudle Glen – was opened by the Douglas & Laxey Coast Electric Tramway Co on 7 September 1893.
Phil Tatt/Online Transport Archive

Situated between Groudle Glen and Baldrine is the MER halt at Baldromma Beg, which is sometimes known as Halfway House after the local public house. Immediately to the north of the halt there are two level crossings; the southernmost of the two is that across King Edward Road whilst the second, historically controlled as seen in this view by traffic lights, crosses the main Douglas to Laxey road. Pictured at the crossing with a service heading towards Douglas is 1894-built No 7. For a number of years No 7 was relegated to engineering duties and its condition deteriorated; however, it was fully restored in 2010 and again now forms part of the operational fleet. The crossing of the main A2 remains light controlled, although the equipment has been upgraded since 1956.
Phil Tatt/Online Transport Archive

As the MER skirts around the perimeter of the King Edward Bay Golf Club, the trams run alongside King Edward Road. In August 1953, No 33 is seen again, this time descending past the Howstrake Holiday Camp as the conductor makes his way to collect the fares. The passengers on the front vestibule have a perfect view of the driver at work and of the approaches to Douglas from the north.
Phil Tatt/Online Transport Archive

During August 1956 Nos 19 and 45 are seen descending from Onchan Head towards the terminus at Derby Castle. No 19 was one of the four 'Winter Saloons' supplied by G. F. Milnes & Co in 1899 for the opening of the Laxey to Ramsey section; five trailers – Nos 44-48 – were supplied by the same manufacturer simultaneously. Although Nos 46–48 remain part of the operation, No 44 was destroyed in the Laxey fire of 1930 and No 45, which had been involved in a derailment at Ballaglass Glen in August 1944 (and subsequently rebuilt at Derby Castle), remained in service until 2000 when withdrawn for an overhaul. However, it was decided to remove the body and convert the trailer into a flat wagon for use by the Permanent Way department. It emerged in this new guise in 2004 and is now largely based at Laxey for maintenance work. The removed body remains in store at Derby Castle and so the tram could be restored to its original condition if desired.
Phil Tatt/Online Transport Archive

One of the original three power cars supplied by G. F. Milnes & Co of Birkenhead for the MER's opening in 1893, No 2 is seen with crossbench trailer No 54 at Derby Castle in August 1953. All three were equipped with Brush D type bogies and could accommodate 34 seated passengers. No 3 was one of the trams destroyed in the Laxey depot fire of 1930 whilst Nos 1 and 2 were relegated to works cars for many years. In 1979, as part of the celebrations of the millennium of Tynwald, both 1 and 2 were fully restored to their original condition and both remain part of the MER's current operational fleet. No 54 was one of the six trailers supplied again by G. F. Milnes for the opening of the line; these were originally numbered 11-16, but became Nos 23-28 in 1895; there were finally renumbered to 49-54 during 1903 and 1904. Of the six, Nos 51 and 54 are part of the operational fleet (having been restored in 2018 and 2019 respectively), whilst No 52 has lost its body (converted into a flatbed runner) and Nos 49, 50 and 53 are in store (having been withdrawn in 2001, 1978 and 1977 respectively). *Phil Tatt/Online Transport Archive*

The MER possessed three depots; the largest of the trio was that situated at Derby Castle. This depot is seen here in August 1953; the structure was to remain largely intact until 1997 when the depot illustrated here – the old top shed – was demolished and replaced. Amongst trams visible are trailer No 50 (one of six supplied by G. F. Milnes & Co for the line's opening in 1893), No 28 (one of a quartet supplied by the Electric Railway & Tramway Carriage Works in 1904), No 33 (one of two crossbench cars built by the United Electric Car Co in 1906) and No 57 (one of two trailers also supplied in 1904 by the Electric Railway & Tramway Carriage Works).
Phil Tatt/Online Transport Archive

On 12 June 1956 MER No 9 stands at the line's southern terminus – Derby Castle. No 9 was the last of the batch of six cars acquired from G. F. Milnes & Co in 1894 for the opening of the line to Laxey. In 1993 this tram was selected to become an illuminated car, being fitted with external rope lights for the purpose. It remains in this condition and is part of the MER's operational fleet. *Julian Thompson/Online Transport Archive*

During the summer of 1956, Douglas No 27 is eased into the depot at Strathallan Crescent. The depot opened in 1896 to replace an earlier depot at Burnt Hill Mill in the town centre. The depot was modified on several occasions: during the first decade of the 20th century, during the 1920s and again in the 1930s. In 2016 a structural survey indicated that the original building was life expired and, two years later, planning consent was given for a new building – designed to replicate the original – to be constructed; this was completed in June 2020. No 27 was one of three 30-seat winter saloons supplied by G. F. Milnes & Co in 1892. Although Nos 27 and 29 remain part of the operational, No 28 was sold off – for £2,800 – in August 2016.
Phil Tatt/Online Transport Archive

With Strathallan Crescent depot to the left, Douglas No 45 is seen during August 1953 departing from Derby Castle as No 36 stands in front of the depot. No 45 was one of three covered toastracks – Nos 45-47 – that were built between 1909 and 1911 by Milnes Voss & Co. Of the trio, No 45 is the only one that remains in service. No 46 was withdrawn in 1987 and preserved in England; latterly it was based in Birkenhead, but was scrapped in 2001. No 47 was withdrawn in 1978 and preserved on the island; it is now based at the transport museum at Jurby. No 36 was one of six trams – Nos 32-37 – that were again supplied by G. F. Milnes & Co, this time in 1896, in order to supplement the fleet. Of the six, No 36 was the only one to be enlarged – in 1908 – taking its seating capacity from 32 to 40 and is the only one remaining in regular service, having received a rebuild in 2017. No 32 remains as part of the operator's heritage fleet with No 35 now displayed at the Bulrhenny home for retired horses. The remaining three were all sold at auction in August 2016 but remain on the island.
Phil Tatt/Online Transport Archive

Also seen departing from Derby Castle is No 50; this was one of three trams – Nos 48-50 – that were the last new trams to be acquired for the horse tramway. Built by the Vulcan Motor & Engineering Co of Southport, the three cars were new in 1935 as convertible saloons. All three were rebuilt into all-weather cars in 1979 in order to be able to operate a five minute frequency of service during inclement weather. However, they were not to survive long in this guise, being sold the following year to the MER for conversion into platform shelters. Of the three, only No 49 was so used with Nos 48 and 50 being scrapped. The remains of No 49 were rescued for display in Ramsey in 1982.
Phil Tatt/Online Transport Archive

During August 1956, No 34 is pictured at Victoria Pier as the conductor leads the horse around the tram at the terminus. Behind the tram can be seen the original Victorian arcade that served Victoria Pier; this structure was not to survive the decade for long – it was demolished in late 1961 prior to the construction of the new ferry terminal. Victoria Pier itself was built to provide extra capacity in the mid-19th century as the number of visitors increased and the existing harbour facilities proved inadequate. The new pier was opened on 1 July 1872 by Henry Loch, the island's then Lieutenant Governor. It was subsequently extended by a further 400ft. No 34 was one of the trams sold at auction in August 2016. Following the sale, No 34 was preserved at the Isle of Man Motor Museum at Jurby, where it has been restored. Now fitted with an engine, steering wheel and rubber tyres, the vehicle is now capable of being driven on the road.
Phil Tatt/Online Transport Archive

In August 1953 Douglas No 40 awaits departure from Victoria Pier. This was one of three open toastrack cars – Nos 38-40 – that were built by G. F. Milnes & Co in 1905. Designed to accommodate 40 passengers, the trio survived until August 2016. Although No 38 was retained as part of the operational fleet, Nos 39 and 40 were sold at auction. The former was sold for £1,800 to the Manx Electric Railway Society whilst the latter was sold privately for £1,000; both, however, remain on the island.
Phil Tatt/Online Transport Archive

A horse tramway needs horses and so stables are required to accommodate them and here, during the summer of 1956, horses are being led out through the yard entrance. The stables, situated behind Tramway Terrace, were originally developed in 1877 when accommodation for 20 horses was provided; by 1902 the capacity had increased to 33 with additional horses being stabled at Strathallan Crescent. The stables, which are now on the Manx Protected Buildings Register, remain in use. Amongst the facilities on site is the smithy; each horse used requires reshoeing approximately every four weeks depending on usage.
Phil Tatt/Online Transport Archive

With the harbour as backdrop and the broad sweep of the town stretching around Douglas Bay in the background, one of the two toastrack cars used on the Douglas Head Funicular Railway can be seen during the summer of 1953. The short line, which ran from the foot of Douglas Head to the summit, near to the site of the camera obscura, opened in 1896 during the period when the island was becoming an increasingly popular holiday destination and was designed to provide a link from the Pier to the Douglas Southern Electric Tramway. The Isle of Man Steam Packet Co ferries visible are *Ben-my-Cree* (stern only), *Snaefell*, *Tynwald* and *Lady of Mann*.
Phil Tatt/Online Transport Archive

The lower terminus of the Douglas Head Funicular Railway pictured during the summer of 1953. The line extended over a distance of 137m with an average gradient of 1 in 4½ and a track gauge of 1,219mm. By this date the line, which had closed during World War 2 but reopened in 1949, was approaching its demise; the reduction in the facilities at Douglas Head allied to the decline in the popularity of the island as a holiday destination and the rise of bus competition saw the line closed completely in 1954 and dismantled. Although little now remains, it is possible to trace the route of the line up the hillside. The Douglas Head Funicular Railway was one of five cliff lifts that served the island at various times. The other four saw two serve – at different times – the Falcon Cliff Hotel in Douglas (the more recent is still extant albeit not used since 1990), one at Port Soderick (which was the original one serving the Falcon Cliff Hotel but relocated) and one linking Laxey with Bowside. *Phil Tatt/Online Transport Archive*

The 2ft 0in gauge Groudle Glen Railway, which was promoted by Richard Maltby Broadbent (who owned the land over which it was built), originally opened on 23 May 1896 to provide a link through the glen from the newly opened Manx Electric Railway to Sea Lion Rocks, where a zoo was established. Services were suspended during both World Wars and, when this view was recorded on 9 April 1950, services had not been reintroduced since the end of the war. The zoo never reopened and the railway was curtailed slightly by a landslip. After some 11 years of disuse, the buildings at the Sea Lion Rocks terminus are in need of some attention. *Tony Wickens/Online Transport Archive*

It's the summer of 1956 and the Groudle Glen Railway is back in operation as one of its W. G. Bagnall-built 2-4-0Ts – *Polar Bear* – heads towards Sea Lion Rocks. The first of the duo – *Sea Lion* – was built for the line's opening in 1896 with the second – *Polar Bear* – following in 1905. Although both locomotives survived in 1950, the line reopened using *Polar Bear* as *Sea Lion* had been stored in the open and so was in a poor condition. The line's operation during the 1950s was variable and all services ceased at the end of the 1962 season but the line and equipment was left moribund. *Polar Bear* was secured for preservation and transferred to the Amberley Working Museum, where it was restored, whilst *Sea Lion* also moved to England. However, *Sea Lion* was fully restored in the late 1980s and returned to the island in 1987 for operation over the reopened railway.
Phil Tatt/Online Transport Archive

Designed by Sir John Coode and built by Head Wrighton, the 2,241ft-long Queen's Pier at Ramsey was constructed for the Isle of Man Harbour Board and opened on 22 July 1886. To assist in the construction of the pier, a 3ft 0in gauge tramway was constructed along the structure. It was initially intended that this would be removed when the pier was completed but, with the addition of passing loops and sidings, the line was retained to facilitate the movement of passengers and luggage along the pier to connect with the steamers for which it was designed to serve.

In August 1950 a Wickham railcar was acquired to supplement the existing rolling stock; it is pictured here during the spring of 1954 at the landward terminus. Beyond can be seen the two diverging spurs into the road beyond the pier; these were replaced by a short straight section into the road during 1955 and 1956. The Wickham was powered by a Ford 52hp engine; theoretically, this could achieve 20mph although such speeds were rare due to inadequate braking. The entrance to the pier was rebuilt in 1956. *Phil Tatt/Online Transport Archive*

The original rolling stock used on the pier tramway was hand-powered. However, in 1937 a single 'Planet' 0-4-0PM, built by F. C. Hibberd & Co Ltd, was delivered to the tramway; this was fitted with a Ford-built petrol engine and is seen here again in the spring of 1954. The tramway continued to operate until 1990, although the last steamer called at the pier 20 years earlier, and the stock was preserved; the 'Planet' is currently part of the collection held by the Jurby Transport Museum. The condition of the pier was one factor in the decision to close the line but, in 1994, the Friends of Ramsey Queen's Pier was established and initial work on the pier's repair commenced. Significant progress was not achieved, however, until a major restoration commenced in 2015. Once completed, it is the intention that the tramway will be reopened. *Phil Tatt/Online Transport Archive*

The only standard gauge railway or tramway on the island was the 4½-mile long Douglas Southern Electric Tramway that ran along the coast from Douglas southwards to Port Soderick. A subsidiary of the New General Traction Co, the line opened on 2 September 1896. The line was operated by eight power cars – Nos 1-8 – supplied by Brush and eight trailers. The line closed on 25 August 1939 at the end of that year's summer season and never reopened after the war. The assets were sold to the Isle of Man Highways Board and the track and overhead were largely removed between 1946 and 1948. However, the fleet and depot remained intact and were visited by a group of enthusiasts in 1951. Determined that one car should be preserved, the efforts primarily of Keith Pearson saw No 1 secured. It was transferred to the Museum of British Transport at Clapham in 1955. It now forms part of the National Tramway Museum collection at Crich. The remainder of the fleet was not so lucky, as this view of the largely dismantled remains of two of the trailers (Nos 9 and 11) demonstrates.
Marcus Eavis/Online Transport Archive